SMART DIY: BOOK V

Where's the Money Coming From?:

The Honest Guide to Financing Your ADU Without Going Broke

Smart DIY - Volume V

Written by Thomas Quirk
Edited by Angélica Díaz
Review and Design by Angélica Díaz

First Edition: 2026
Production:

SMART DIY: BOOK V

Where's the Money Coming From?:

The Honest Guide to Financing Your ADU Without Going Broke

Content

INTRODUCTION

The $300,000 Question: "How Do I Actually Pay for This?"

For most homeowners, the ADU journey starts with inspiration—a Pinterest board, a vision of rental income, or a place for family—until reality hits hard when the first real estimates arrive at $250,000, $300,000, $400,000 or more, and excitement turns into anxiety around the $300,000 question: "How do I actually pay for this?" If you don't have hundreds of thousands of dollars sitting in a bank account, you are not behind—you are normal, because the vast majority of ADU projects are not funded with cash.

Most homeowners don't abandon ADU plans because they don't want them; they abandon them because the numbers feel overwhelming, financing options sound confusing or risky, and no one clearly explains how the process actually works. This disconnect between the desire to build and the ability to fund it is the single biggest roadblock in the ADU journey, stopping more projects at the financing stage than at permitting or construction. When financing feels opaque, homeowners freeze; when it becomes understandable, projects move forward.

This section of the book is not about abstract financial theory or lender sales pitches, but a practical, plain-language roadmap for funding an ADU in the real world. It strips away lending jargon, explains how ADUs are actually financed today, and walks through the three primary pathways successful homeowners use—tapping existing home equity, using construction or renovation loans, and leveraging the future value of the ADU itself—so you can evaluate the tradeoffs, risks, and use cases and choose what fits your goals and risk tolerance. By reframing the question from "Can I afford this?" to "What's the smartest way to fund this?", the cost stops feeling paralyzing and becomes manageable, transforming the $300,000 question from a source of fear into a problem with clear, achievable solutions and moving you from "I wish I could" to "Here's how I do it."

PART I

THE FOUNDATION OF YOUR FINANCIAL PLAN

CHAPTER 1

WHAT LENDERS SEE: YOUR CREDIT, DTI, AND EQUITY

Before you can secure financing for your ADU, you need to do one important thing:

Stop seeing your finances the way a homeowner does—and start seeing them the way a lender does.

Banks and credit unions don't fund dreams.

They manage **risk**.

To a lender, you are not:

- A homeowner with a vision
- A future landlord
- A planner with good intentions

You are a **set of numbers** that predict whether you will repay a loan.

Homeowners who understand how lenders think walk into financing conversations prepared—and walk out with better terms.

This chapter breaks down the t**hree data points that matter most:**

1. Your **credit score**
2. Your **debt-to-income (DTI) ratio**

3. Your **home equity and loan-to-value (LTV)**

Once you understand these, you can accurately estimate your borrowing power **before** talking to a lender.

1. Your Credit Score: The Gatekeeper

Your credit score is the **first filter** every lender applies.

It's a numerical summary of how reliably you've borrowed and repaid money in the past—and it strongly predicts how risky you are today.

Why It Matters

A higher credit score:

- Unlocks **lower interest rates**
- Expands your loan options
- Can save **tens of thousands of dollars** over the life of a loan

A low score:

- Raises your rate
- Shrinks your options
- May block financing altogether

Interest Rates Are Not Cosmetic

A one-point difference in interest rate can cost more than a kitchen remodel over 30 years.

What Lenders Typically Look For

- **Below ~680 →** Financing becomes difficult
- **700+ →** Access to most competitive products

- **720+ →** Considered "strong" or "excellent"

While some government-backed loans allow lower scores, **720 is the gold standard** for flexible ADU financing.

How to Improve It (Practically)

You improve your score by:

- Paying every bill on time (no exceptions)
- Paying down credit card balances
- Keeping credit utilization low
- Disputing errors on your credit report

Credit score improvement is often the cheapest way to increase borrowing power.

2. Debt-to-Income (DTI): Your Capacity to Carry More Debt

Your DTI ratio answers one question for a lender:

How much of your income is already spoken for?

It compares your monthly debt payments to your monthly gross (pre-tax) income.

How to Calculate DTI

1. ***Add all monthly debt payments:***
    - Mortgage
    - Car loans
    - Student loans
    - Credit card minimums

2. *Divide by your monthly gross income.*

Example:

- Monthly debts: $3,000
- Gross income: $8,000

DTI = **37.5%**

What Lenders Look For

Most lenders cap DTI at:

- **43%–45%**, including the new ADU loan

That means:

If adding the ADU loan pushes you above this threshold, the loan may be denied—even if you have equity.

Equity Alone Is Not Enough: Many homeowners have plenty of equity—but fail DTI.

3. Home Equity & Loan-to-Value (LTV): Your Borrowing Ceiling

Home equity is your **primary collateral** for ADU financing.

How to Calculate Home Equity

Home value

− Current mortgage balance

= Equity

Example:

- Home value: $800,000
- Mortgage balance: $500,000

Equity = **$300,000**

Loan-to-Value (LTV): The Hidden Limit

Lenders won't let you borrow all your equity.

They use **Loan-to-Value (LTV)**:

Total loan amount ÷ home value

Most lenders cap LTV at:

- **80%–85%**

That means:

- Your existing mortgage **plus**
- Your new ADU loan must stay below that percentage.

> **The Silent Disqualifier:** A project can fail financing even with good credit if LTV limits are exceeded.

Why These Three Numbers Work Together

Lenders don't look at these metrics in isolation.

They ask:

- Is your credit strong?
- Can you afford the payments?
- Is there enough collateral?

If **any one** of these fails, financing becomes harder—or more expensive.

The strongest ADU borrowers aren't the wealthiest—they're the most balanced across these three metrics.

What You Should Understand Now

- ☐ Lenders evaluate risk, not vision
- ☐ Credit score affects rates and options
- ☐ DTI limits how much you can borrow
- ☐ Equity is capped by LTV rules
- ☐ Strength in one area can't fully offset weakness in another

Immediate Actions

1. **Check your actual credit score:** Don't guess.
2. **Calculate your current DTI:** Include all debts.
3. **Estimate your current home value conservatively:** Lenders will.
4. **Identify your weakest metric**

That's where improvement pays off fastest.

Scripts You Can Use With Lenders

Script: Starting the Conversation

"I'd like to understand my borrowing power based on credit, DTI, and LTV."

Script: If You're Told "Not Yet"

"What specific metric needs improvement for approval?"

Red-Flag Response

"We'll see what you qualify for after you apply."

You should already have a strong estimate before applying.

Financial Self-Assessment Worksheet

Use this before speaking to any lender.

1. **Credit Score**
   - Estimated Credit Score: ______
   - Action to Improve (if needed): ____________________
2. **Debt-to-Income (DTI)**
   - Monthly Gross Income: $______
   - Monthly Debt Payments: $______
   - My DTI Ratio: ______ %
3. **Home Equity & LTV**
   - Estimated Home Value: $______
   - Current Mortgage Balance: $______
   - Available Equity: $______
   - Maximum Total Loan Amount (85% LTV): $______

Financing an ADU is not about convincing a bank to believe in your dream.

It's about **aligning your numbers with their rules.**

When you understand how lenders see you, financing stops feeling mysterious—and starts feeling **manageable**.

CHAPTER 2

THE ALL-IN BUDGET: HARD COSTS, SOFT COSTS, AND CONTINGENCY

The single most common reason ADU projects fail is not permitting.

It's not contractors.

It's not even financing.

It's an **incomplete budget.**

Most homeowners focus on the visible costs—the concrete, lumber, and finishes—while dramatically underestimating the less obvious expenses and completely ignoring the need for a contingency fund.

That mistake doesn't just cause stress.

It makes financing impossible.

In real ADU projects, lenders don't reject borrowers because they lack vision—they reject them because the budget doesn't reflect reality.

A successful financing plan can only be built on a realistic, all-in budget. This chapter shows you how to build one—honestly, completely, and defensibly.

Hard Costs: The Bricks and Mortar

Hard costs are the expenses tied directly to the physical construction of the ADU. These are the costs most people instinctively think of—and they do make up the largest portion of the budget.

Typical hard costs include:

- **Foundation:** Concrete, rebar, excavation, and labor
- **Framing:** Lumber, sheathing, structural hardware, labor
- **Exterior Finishes:** Siding, roofing, windows, doors
- **Interior Finishes:** Drywall, flooring, paint, trim
- **Mechanical, Electrical & Plumbing (MEP):** Wiring, piping, HVAC systems
- **Kitchen & Bath:** Cabinets, countertops, fixtures, appliances

The Trap: Hard costs feel like "the budget," but they are only one piece of it.

Hard costs may dominate the spreadsheet, but **they do not tell the whole story**—and lenders know it.

Soft Costs: The Invisible Budget Killers

Soft costs are the non-physical, service-based expenses required to legally design, permit, and manage your ADU.

They are essential. They are unavoidable. And they are routinely underestimated.

Common soft costs include:

- Architectural design
- Structural engineering
- Title 24 / energy compliance
- Surveying and soils reports
- Permit and plan check fees
- Utility connection and capacity fees
- School, park, or impact fees
- Insurance and inspections
- Financing fees and interest during construction

In Southern California, soft costs alone often total **$30,000–$80,000+.**

Failing to include soft costs doesn't make the project cheaper.

It just guarantees **budget shock later**—often after financing is already locked in.

Contingency: The Non-Negotiable Safety Net

No construction project goes exactly as planned.
Ever.

Unexpected conditions, price changes, and mid-project decisions are not signs of failure—they are **normal**. The only difference between a successful project and a financial disaster is whether you planned for them.

That's what contingency is for.

What a Contingency Fund Is

A contingency fund is:

- **A separate reserve of money**
- Set aside specifically for the unexpected
- Not part of your day-to-day budget

It is not optional.

How Much You Need

Industry standard:

- **10%–15% of the total project cost:** (Hard + Soft Costs)

Example:

- $300,000 total project
- Contingency required: $30,000–$45,000

> **Lender Reality:** If your budget has no contingency, lenders assume you will run out of money.

What Contingency Covers

- **Unforeseen site conditions:** (e.g., cracked sewer lateral)
- **Material price increases:** (e.g., lumber or concrete spikes)
- **Change orders:** (upgraded finishes, added windows, design tweaks)

The Only Budget That Matters: All-In Cost

Your true ADU budget is not the contractor's bid.

It is:

****Hard Costs**

- Soft Costs
- Contingency
- = All-In Budget**

Only when you have realistic numbers for **all three** can you:

- Approach lenders confidently
- Avoid mid-project panic
- Make informed design decisions

> **Financing Rule:** You don't finance "construction."
> You finance the **entire project.**

Is Your Budget Lender-Ready?

- ☐ Hard costs are fully itemized
- ☐ Soft costs are included and realistic
- ☐ Utility and permit fees are accounted for
- ☐ Contingency fund is 10–15%
- ☐ Total budget reflects real cash needs

If any box is unchecked, your budget is incomplete.

Immediate Actions

1. **Separate hard and soft costs clearly:** Don't lump them together.
2. **Add contingency as its own line item:** Not "extra," not "optional."
3. **Stress-test your total number:** Ask: *Can I survive if costs hit this number?*
4. **Use this all-in number for financing conversations:** Not the contractor's bid.

Scripts You Can Use With Lenders or Designers

Script: With a Lender

"This is my all-in ADU budget, including soft costs and contingency."

Script: With a Contractor

"Your bid is one part of my total project budget—what's not included here?"

Script: With Yourself

"If I can't fund the full budget, I'm not ready to build."

That honesty saves projects.

Sample ADU Budget Framework (Simplified)

- Hard Costs: $________
- Soft Costs: $________
- Contingency (10–15%): $________

Total All-In Budget: $________

A realistic budget doesn't make your ADU more expensive. It makes it **possible**.

When your numbers reflect reality, financing becomes smoother, decisions become clearer, and stress drops dramatically. This is the foundation every successful ADU project is built on—and every lender expects to see.

Hope is not a budget. **Precision is.**

CHAPTER 3

THE APPRAISAL GAP: WHY YOUR ADU ISN'T WORTH ITS COST (AT FIRST)

One of the most confusing—and frustrating—realities of ADU financing is something lenders call **the appraisal gap.**

This gap is the difference between:

- **What it costs you to build the ADU**
- **What an appraiser says your property is worth afterward**

Understanding this gap is critical, because it directly limits how much you can borrow using traditional, equity-based financing.

Many well-planned ADU projects stall not because they are unaffordable—but because the appraisal math doesn't work the way homeowners expect.

This chapter explains **why the appraisal gap exists, how it affects borrowing, and what it means for your financing strategy.**

Cost vs. Value: Two Numbers That Are Not the Same

In a perfectly logical world, spending $300,000 on an ADU would increase your property value by $300,000.

That is **not how real estate appraisal works.**

The Two Numbers That Matter

- **Cost:** What you actually spend on the ADU (Hard costs + soft costs)
- **Value:** What a buyer would pay for your property with the ADU (As determined by a licensed appraiser)

In many Southern California markets:

- **A $300,000 ADU**
- May add only **$150,000–$200,000** in immediate appraised value

That difference—often **$100,000–$150,000**—is the **appraisal gap.**

The Emotional Trap: "I spent it, so it must be worth it" is emotionally true—but financially irrelevant to a lender.

Why the Appraisal Gap Exists: The Tyranny of "Comps"

Appraisers don't assign value based on effort, quality, or cost.

They assign value based on **comparable sales**, called **"comps."**

What Are Comps?

Comps are recent sales of:

- Similar homes
- In the same neighborhood
- With similar features

To value your ADU, an appraiser must find **other homes that sold with ADUs.**

That's where the problem begins.

The Core Problem: Not Enough ADU Comps

In many neighborhoods:

- ADUs are still relatively new
- Few comparable sales exist
- Data is thin or inconsistent

Appraisers are not allowed to "guess" or assume value.

They must **justify every adjustment with market data.**

Why Appraisers Are Conservative: When data is limited, appraisers protect themselves by valuing cautiously—not optimistically.

Cost Approach vs. Sales Comparison Approach

Appraisers may consider what it cost to build your ADU (the **cost approach**), but they are usually required to rely primarily on the sales comparison approach.

When comps are scarce:

- Adjustments are conservative
- Value increases are muted
- Appraisal gaps appear

This is not personal. It's procedural.

How the Appraisal Gap Restricts Traditional Financing

The appraisal gap matters because **most traditional ADU financing is equity-based.**

Loans like:

- HELOCs
- Cash-out refinances

are based on the **current appraised value of your home**—before the ADU exists.

A Real-World Example

- Home value (before ADU): **$800,000**
- Current mortgage balance: **$500,000**
- Total equity: **$300,000**

Most lenders cap borrowing at **85% loan-to-value (LTV).**

- 85% of $800,000 = **$680,000**

- $680,000 – $500,000 = **$180,000 max loan**

But your ADU costs **$300,000.**

Shortfall: $120,000

> This is the appraisal gap in action. Banks lend against today's value—not tomorrow's potential.

Why This Is So Frustrating for Homeowners

From your perspective:

- You know the ADU will generate income
- You know it improves long-term value
- You know it's a smart investment

From the lender's perspective:

- That value is not proven yet
- Rental income may not exist yet
- The ADU is not part of the appraisal yet

Both perspectives are valid—but only one controls loan approval.

Closing the Gap: Why Future Income Changes Everything

The appraisal gap is a major obstacle—but not an unsolvable one.

Newer ADU-specific financing products have emerged specifically to address this problem.

These loans may:

- Consider **future rental income**
- Adjust **DTI calculations** using projected rent
- Underwrite based on **post-construction value**, not just current value

By recognizing the ADU as an **income-producing** asset, these products can justify:

- Larger loan amounts
- Smaller upfront cash requirements

Financing products that account for future rental income are expanding access to ADUs for homeowners who would otherwise be blocked by the appraisal gap.

(We'll explore these options in detail in the next section.)

What You Should Understand Now

- ☐ Cost and value are not the same
- ☐ Appraisal gaps are normal—not a failure
- ☐ Appraisers rely on comps, not construction cost
- ☐ Equity-based loans are limited by current value
- ☐ The gap explains many ADU financing rejections

Immediate Actions

1. **Stop assuming cost = value:** Build your financing plan around reality.
2. **Estimate your pre-ADU appraised value conservatively:** Lenders will.

3. **Calculate your equity-based borrowing limit:** Before committing to a design.
4. **Accept that one loan type may not solve everything:** Hybrid strategies are common.

Scripts You Can Use With Lenders

Script: Asking the Right Question

"Is this loan based on current appraised value or post-construction value?"

Script: When You Hear "You Don't Have Enough Equity"

"What financing options consider future rental income from the ADU?"

Red-Flag Explanation

"The ADU will be worth it later—trust us."

Lenders don't finance trust. They finance structure.

The appraisal gap isn't a punishment.

It's a **timing issue.**

Traditional financing looks backward. ADUs create value forward.

Once you understand that mismatch, the problem stops feeling mysterious—and starts feeling **strategic**.

PART II

TAPPING INTO YOUR EXISTING HOME EQUITY

CHAPTER 4

THE HOME EQUITY LINE OF CREDIT (HELOC): YOUR FLEXIBLE FRIEND

For homeowners with meaningful home equity, the **Home Equity Line of Credit (HELOC)** is the most popular way to finance an ADU—and for good reason.

A HELOC is **not** a lump-sum loan.

It is a **revolving line of credit,** similar to a credit card, that is secured by your home.

That flexibility makes it especially well-suited to construction, where costs arrive in stages and rarely on a neat schedule.

Among experienced ADU homeowners, the HELOC is often the tool of choice—but only when used with discipline.

This chapter explains **how a HELOC works, why it fits construction so well, and where it can quietly go wrong.**

How a HELOC Works: Two Phases You Must Understand

A HELOC always has **two distinct phases.** Confusing them is where many homeowners get burned.

Phase 1: The Draw Period (Usually 10 Years)

This is the construction-friendly phase.

During the draw period:

- You can borrow up to your approved limit
- You can draw funds **as needed,** repay, and draw again
- You only pay interest on the amount you've actually borrowed

This matches how construction works:

- Contractor invoices arrive in stages
- Costs vary month to month
- Cash flow is uneven

Why HELOCs Fit Construction: You're not paying interest on money you haven't used yet.

In most cases, payments during the draw period are **interest-only,** keeping monthly obligations lower while construction is underway.

Phase 2: The Repayment Period (15–20 Years)

Once the draw period ends:

- You can no longer borrow from the line
- The balance converts to a traditional loan
- You begin paying **principal + interest**

This is where planning matters.

If you haven't prepared for this transition, the monthly payment increase can be jarring.

Most HELOC problems don't appear during construction—they appear years later when the repayment phase begins.

Why Homeowners Like HELOCs: The Real Advantages

The HELOC is popular because it solves several common ADU financing problems elegantly.

1. Flexibility (The Biggest Advantage)

You only borrow what you need, when you need it.

That means:

- No interest on unused funds
- Easier alignment with construction draws
- Better control of cash flow

2. Lower Payments During Construction

Interest-only payments during the draw period:

- Reduce financial pressure
- Preserve cash for unexpected costs
- Pair well with a contingency fund

This matters during months when:

- Rent hasn't started
- Expenses are peaking

3. Lower Closing Costs

Compared to:

- Cash-out refinances

- Construction loans

HELOCs usually have:

- Lower fees
- Faster approval
- Less paperwork

HELOC Efficiency: For homeowners who already have equity, a HELOC is often the cheapest way to access it.

Where HELOCs Go Wrong: The Real Risks

A HELOC is powerful—but it is not harmless.

1. Variable Interest Rates

Most HELOCs are tied to a benchmark like the **Prime Rate.**

That means:

- If rates rise, your payment rises
- Budget certainty is reduced
- Long-term costs are unpredictable

This isn't a problem if you plan for it. **It is a problem if you ignore it.**

2. The Temptation to Overspend

Easy access to money creates risk.

Common mistakes:

- Upgrading finishes impulsively
- Using HELOC funds for non-ADU expenses
- Treating the credit line as "extra money"

Discipline Is the Price of Flexibility. A HELOC doesn't overspend—you do.

3. Payment Shock at Conversion

When the draw period ends:

- Interest-only payments stop
- Principal repayment begins
- Monthly payments can jump sharply

If your ADU rental income isn't stable by then—or if rates have increased—this can strain your finances.

The best HELOC users plan their exit strategy before they draw their first dollar.

Who a HELOC Is Best For (and Who It Isn't)

A HELOC works best for homeowners who:

- Have **strong equity**
- Have **stable income**
- Are financially disciplined

- Understand interest-rate risk

It is **not ideal** for homeowners who:

- Need fixed payments for peace of mind
- Are already stretched on monthly obligations
- Tend to overspend when funds are accessible

Is a HELOC Right for You?

- ☐ I have sufficient home equity
- ☐ I understand variable-rate risk
- ☐ I can manage interest-only payments responsibly
- ☐ I have a plan for repayment-period payments
- ☐ I will restrict HELOC use to the ADU project

If any box is unchecked, pause before proceeding.

Immediate Actions

1. **Confirm your HELOC borrowing limit:** Based on LTV rules—not assumptions.
2. **Ask how the rate is calculated:** Prime + what?
3. **Model the repayment-period payment:** Don't guess—calculate.
4. **Set spending rules for yourself.** Treat HELOC funds as restricted capital.

Scripts You Can Use With Lenders

Script: Understanding the Risk

"What happens to my payment if rates rise by two percentage points?"

Script: Planning Ahead

"Can you show me the estimated payment once the draw period ends?"

Script: Staying Disciplined

"This HELOC will be used only for ADU construction expenses."

Red-Flag Thought

"I'll worry about repayment later."

That's when HELOCs become problems instead of tools.

A HELOC is neither good nor bad.

It is **powerful**.

Used thoughtfully, it is one of the most efficient ways to fund an ADU—matching construction cash flow while minimizing early costs.

Used carelessly, it quietly converts flexibility into long-term stress.

The difference is not the loan.

It's the plan behind it.

CHAPTER 5

THE CASH-OUT REFINANCE: LOCKING IN A FIXED RATE

For homeowners who value **predictability and stability over flexibility**, the **cash-out refinance** is the most straightforward alternative to a HELOC.

A cash-out refinance replaces your existing mortgage with a new, larger one—and gives you the difference in cash. Unlike a HELOC, this option lets you **lock in a fixed interest rate** for the entire term of the loan, creating long-term certainty in a way variable-rate options cannot.

Some homeowners sleep better knowing exactly what their payment will be for the next 15 or 30 years—and that peace of mind has real value.

This chapter explains **how a cash-out refinance works, when it makes sense, and when it can quietly cost you far more than expected.**

How a Cash-Out Refinance Works (Step by Step)

The mechanics are simple—but the implications are big.

1. Appraisal

Your lender orders an appraisal to determine your home's **current market value.**

2. New Mortgage Approval

You are approved for a new mortgage that is larger than your current one. Most lenders cap the new loan at **80%–85% loan-to-value (LTV).**

3. Old Mortgage Is Paid Off

At closing, the new mortgage pays off your existing loan in full.

4. You Receive the Cash

The remaining funds—the "cash out"—are deposited into your bank account as a **lump sum.**

Example

- Home value: **$800,000**
- Current mortgage balance: **$400,000**
- New mortgage (80% LTV): **$640,000**

Result:

- Old mortgage paid off: $400,000
- Cash received: **$240,000**

That $240,000 can then be used to fund your ADU.

Key Difference from a HELOC. You receive all the money at once—and you start paying interest on all of it immediately.

Why Homeowners Choose a Cash-Out Refinance

The appeal of a cash-out refinance is rooted in certainty and simplicity.

1. Fixed Interest Rate (The Big Advantage)

Your rate and monthly payment are:

- Locked in
- Predictable
- Immune to future rate hikes

This eliminates the long-term uncertainty that comes with variable-rate loans.

For risk-averse homeowners, payment certainty is often worth more than flexibility.

2. One Simple Monthly Payment

Instead of:

- A mortgage payment **plus**
- A HELOC payment

You have **one consolidated mortgage payment.**

That simplicity:

- Reduces mental load
- Makes budgeting easier
- Lowers the chance of missed payments

3. Possible Rate Improvement (In Specific Situations)

If current mortgage rates are **lower than your existing rate,** a cash-out refinance can:

- Lower the rate on your entire balance
- Offset some of the costs of refinancing

This scenario is increasingly rare—but powerful when it exists.

The Hidden Costs and Real Risks

Despite its stability, a cash-out refinance is not always the smart move.

1. High Closing Costs

This is a **full mortgage refinance**, which means:

- Appraisal fees
- Title insurance
- Loan origination fees
- Escrow and recording fees

Typical cost:

- **2%–5% of the new loan amount**

On a $600,000 mortgage, that's **$12,000–$30,000**—paid up-front or rolled into the loan.

HELOC vs. Cash-Out. HELOCs are cheaper to open.

> Cash-out refinances are more expensive—but more predictable.

2. Giving Up a Historically Low Rate

If your current mortgage was originated during:

- 2020–2021
- Or any unusually low-rate period

Refinancing now could mean:

- Replacing a 2.75% loan
- With a 6%+ loan
- On **your entire mortgage balance**

That can dramatically increase lifetime interest costs.

Many homeowners regret refinancing—not because the ADU failed, but because they gave up an exceptional mortgage rate.

3. Resetting the Clock

A new 30-year mortgage means:

- Your loan term starts over
- More years paying interest
- Higher total interest paid over time

Even with a reasonable rate, this can be costly in the long run.

Who a Cash-Out Refinance Is Best For

A cash-out refinance is often a good fit if you:

- Strongly prefer **fixed payments**
- Don't want interest-rate risk
- Are comfortable paying higher closing costs
- Have a mortgage rate that is not dramatically lower

than today's rates

It may be a **poor fit** if you:

- Have an exceptionally low existing rate
- Need staged access to funds
- Want to minimize upfront costs

Is a Cash-Out Refinance Right for You?

☐ I value long-term payment certainty

☐ I'm comfortable receiving funds as a lump sum

☐ I understand the closing costs involved

☐ I've compared my current rate to today's rates

☐ I'm okay resetting my mortgage term

If **several boxes are unchecked**, explore alternatives before committing.

Immediate Actions

1. **Find your current mortgage rate.** This determines whether refinancing even makes sense.
2. **Request a refinance cost estimate.** Don't guess—ask for real numbers.
3. **Compare lifetime interest, not just monthly payments**
4. **Stress-test your budget with the new payment**

Scripts You Can Use With Lenders

Script: Comparing Options

"What is the total cost difference between keeping my current mortgage and refinancing?"

Script: Rate Reality Check

"How much more interest will I pay over time if I reset to a new 30-year loan?"

Script: Discipline Reminder

"This cash-out will be used only for ADU construction."

Red-Flag Thought

"I'll make up the difference with rent."

Hope is not a strategy—numbers are.

A cash-out refinance trades **flexibility for certainty.**

For the right homeowner, it creates a calm, predictable financial foundation for an ADU. For the wrong one, it quietly increases long-term costs in ways that aren't obvious upfront.

The loan itself isn't good or bad.

The wisdom lies in knowing **which risk you're choosing to eliminate—and which one you're accepting instead.**

CHAPTER 6

HELOC VS. CASH-OUT REFI: A HEAD-TO-HEAD COMPARISON

Choosing between a **Home Equity Line of Credit (HELOC)** and a **cash-out refinance** is one of the most important financial decisions in your ADU journey.

There is **no universally correct answer.**

The right choice depends on:

- Your current mortgage rate
- Your tolerance for risk
- Your need for flexibility vs. certainty
- Your financial discipline

Smart ADU financing isn't about picking the "best" loan—it's about picking the one that fits your reality.

This chapter puts the two options **head-to-heads**, so you can decide with clarity instead of guesswork.

The Side-by-Side Comparison

HELOC vs. Cash-Out Refinance (At a Glance)

Feature	HELOC	Cash-Out Refinance
Interest Rate	Variable	Fixed
Payment Predictability	Low–Medium	High
Access to Funds	As needed (draws)	Lump sum
Best for Construction	Excellent	Moderate
Closing Costs	Low	High (2–5%)
Risk if Rates Rise	Yes	No
Temptation to Over-spend	Higher	Lower
Keeps Existing Mortgage Rate	Yes	No
Monthly Payments During Build	Lower (interest-only)	Higher

The Core Tradeoff

HELOC = flexibility with uncertainty

Cash-out refinance = certainty with commitment

When a HELOC Is the Clear Winner

A HELOC is often the smarter choice if **any** of the following apply:

You Have an Excellent Existing Mortgage Rate

If your current mortgage is in the **2%–3% range,** replacing it would be extremely expensive. A HELOC lets you:

- Keep that low rate

- Borrow only what you need for the ADU
- Avoid resetting your entire mortgage

You Plan to Pay the Loan Down Aggressively

If you intend to:

- Use ADU rental income to pay down debt quickly
- Refinance or convert later
- Keep balances low

Then HELOC flexibility and lower upfront costs are major advantages.

You're Comfortable With Some Risk

If you:

- Understand variable rates
- Can absorb payment fluctuations
- Have financial buffer

A HELOC may be worth the uncertainty.

Many experienced ADU builders use HELOCs strategically—and exit them quickly.

When a Cash-Out Refinance Is the Better Choice

A cash-out refinance often makes sense if s**tability matters more than flexibility.**

You Want Fixed, Predictable Payments

If payment certainty is a priority:

- Fixed rate
- Fixed payment
- No surprises

A cash-out refinance delivers peace of mind a HELOC never can.

Current Rates Are Equal to or Lower Than Your Existing Rate

If refinancing doesn't mean giving up a great rate—or actually improves it—you may:

- Simplify your finances
- Lock in long-term stability
- Reduce overall interest costs

You Need a Large Lump Sum

For larger ADU projects:

- Receiving all funds upfront
- Simplifying accounting
- Avoiding draw management

can make the process easier to manage.

Stability Has a Cost—and a Value. You pay more upfront for certainty, but some homeowners gladly do.

The Decision Tree (Use This)

Answer these questions in order:

1. What Is Your Current Mortgage Rate?

- **Much lower than today's rates** → Lean HELOC
- **Similar or higher than today's rates** → Cash-out refinance is viable

2. How Do You Feel About Risk?

- **Comfortable with variability** → HELOC
- **Strongly prefer certainty** → Cash-out refinance

3. How Disciplined Are You With Money?

- **Highly disciplined, project-only spending** → HELOC
- **Concerned about overspending** → Cash-out refinance

Personality Matters. The wrong loan for your temperament becomes expensive—even if the math looked good.

Are You Choosing Intentionally?

- ☐ I know my current mortgage rate
- ☐ I understand how rates could affect payments
- ☐ I've compared total costs—not just monthly payments
- ☐ I'm honest about my spending discipline
- ☐ I've stress-tested my budget under worst-case scenarios

If any box is unchecked, pause before committing.

Immediate Actions

1. **Write down your current mortgage rate**
2. **Ask lenders for both options—not just one**
3. **Calculate worst-case payments for each**
4. **Decide which risk you're willing to live with**

Not eliminating risk—**choosing it.**

Scripts You Can Use With Lenders

Script: Neutral Comparison

"Can you show me both a HELOC and a cash-out refinance scenario side by side?"

Script: Rate Reality Check

"What happens to my payment if HELOC rates increase by two points?"

Script: Discipline Guardrail

"This financing will be used only for ADU construction."

Red-Flag Advice

"This option is always better."

There is no "always" in financing.

This decision isn't about which loan is smarter in theory.

It's about:

- How you handle uncertainty

- How you manage money under pressure
- What lets you sleep at night

Choose the tool that fits **your numbers and your nature**—and your ADU will be built on a financial foundation you can live with.

PART III

CONSTRUCTION-SPECIFIC FINANCING

CHAPTER 7

THE CONSTRUCTION LOAN: FUNDING YOUR BUILD IN DRAWS

For homeowners who don't have enough existing equity to fund an ADU with a HELOC or cash-out refinance, the **construction loan** is the most powerful—and misunderstood—financing option.

Unlike equity-based loans that look **backward** at what your home is worth today, a construction loan looks **forward**. It bases the loan amount on what your property will be worth **after the ADU is completed.**

That single difference is why construction loans are the primary tool for overcoming the **appraisal gap.**

When equity-based financing hits a wall, construction loans open a door.

This chapter explains **how construction loans actually work, why banks are willing to lend more, and what extra structure and scrutiny come with that power.**

How a Construction Loan Works: The "As-Completed" Appraisal

The foundation of a construction loan is the future value appraisal, often called an **"as-completed" appraisal.**

Here's how the process works in practice:

1. Plans and All-In Budget

You submit:

- A complete set of architectural plans
- A detailed, realistic construction budget
- Contractor information

Incomplete plans = no loan.

2. As-Completed Appraisal

The lender hires an appraiser to answer one question:

What will this property be worth once the ADU is built exactly as shown?

The appraiser uses:

- Your plans
- Your budget
- Local market data and comparable properties

This appraisal is **hypothetical—but regulated.**

This Is the Breakthrough. The bank isn't lending on what exists today—it's lending on what will exist tomorrow.

3. Loan Amount

The lender typically approves:

- **75%–80% of the future appraised value**

This often results in:

- A significantly higher loan amount
- Enough funding to cover most or all of the ADU cost

This is how construction loans solve the **appraisal gap.**

How You Get Paid: The Draw Schedule

A construction loan does **not** give you a lump sum of cash.

Instead, funds are released in stages—called **draws**—as construction progresses.

A typical draw schedule may look like:

- Foundation complete
- Framing complete
- Rough MEP (plumbing, electrical, HVAC)
- Drywall complete
- Final inspection

Before each draw:

- The bank sends its own inspector
- Work is verified on-site
- Funds are released only after approval

This third-party inspection protects both the homeowner and the lender—and often improves contractor performance.

Why Construction Loans Are Powerful

Construction loans exist for a reason. They solve problems that other loans can't.

1. Higher Borrowing Limits

Because the loan is based on **future value**, you can often borrow:

- More than your current equity allows
- Enough to fully fund the ADU

This makes construction loans the **go-to option** when HELOCs and refinances fall short.

2. Built-In Oversight and Structure

The draw schedule:

- Prevents large upfront payments
- Ensures work is completed before funds are released
- Reduces risk of contractor abandonment

For many homeowners, this structure is a hidden advantage.

Discipline by Design. Construction loans force financial discipline—even when emotions run high.

The Tradeoffs: Why Construction Loans Are Not for Everyone

With greater power comes greater complexity.

1. A More Demanding Application

Expect:

- Full plans (not concepts)
- Detailed budgets (not estimates)
- More documentation
- Longer approval timelines

This is not a quick loan.

2. Higher Closing Costs

Construction loans are similar to new mortgages:

- Appraisal fees
- Title and escrow
- Origination fees

Costs are significantly higher than HELOCs.

3. Contractor Vetting

The lender must approve your contractor.

They will look for:

- Licensing and insurance
- Experience with similar projects
- Financial stability
- Track record of completing jobs

This can be a deal-breaker if you plan to use:

- An unproven builder
- A friend or family member
- A contractor with limited ADU experience

Banks don't just underwrite you—they underwrite your contractor.

Who a Construction Loan Is Best For

A construction loan is often the right choice if you:

- Don't have sufficient existing equity
- Are blocked by the appraisal gap
- Need to borrow a large amount
- Are willing to accept structure and oversight

It may be a poor fit if you:

- Want speed and simplicity
- Have limited contractor options
- Are uncomfortable with bank inspections

Is a Construction Loan a Fit?

- ☐ I understand this loan is based on future value
- ☐ I have (or can obtain) complete plans
- ☐ I have a qualified contractor
- ☐ I'm comfortable with bank inspections
- ☐ I need more borrowing power than equity allows

If several boxes are unchecked, explore other options first.

Immediate Actions

1. **Confirm your total all-in ADU budget**
2. **Ask lenders if they offer ADU construction loans**
3. **Verify your contractor meets bank requirements**
4. **Prepare for a longer approval timeline**

Planning ahead makes this loan far less stressful.

Scripts You Can Use With Lenders

Script: Opening the Conversation

"Do you offer construction loans based on as-completed value for ADUs?"

Script: Contractor Question

"What qualifications does my contractor need to meet for approval?"

Script: Timeline Check

"What is the realistic approval and funding timeline?"

Red-Flag Answer

"We'll figure that out later."

In construction lending, **later is expensive.**

Construction loans aren't easy—but they are often the **only** path forward when equity-based financing runs out of road.

If you need more borrowing power, are willing to meet stricter requirements, and want a loan aligned with your ADU's **future**

value, the construction loan can turn an impossible project into a feasible one.

It doesn't make the process simpler.

It makes the project possible.

CHAPTER 8

THE RENOVATION LOAN: FHA 203(K) AND FANNIE MAE HOMESTYLE

For some homeowners, the biggest obstacle to building an ADU isn't design or permitting—it's **qualifying for financing.**

If you don't meet the credit score, equity, or down-payment requirements for a HELOC or a traditional construction loan, **government-backed renovation loans** can offer another path forward. Programs like the **FHA 203(k)** and **Fannie Mae HomeStyle** allow you to **bundle the cost of construction into your primary mortgage**, spreading the expense over time.

These loans are not easy—but for the right borrower, they can turn an otherwise blocked project into a viable one.

This chapter explains **how renovation loans work, who they're best for, and what tradeoffs come with the extra access.**

How Renovation Loans Work (In Simple Terms)

Renovation loans share DNA with construction loans—but with a different purpose.

They are designed to:

- Purchase or refinance a home and
- Finance major renovations at the same time

The key idea is this:

Your loan is based on what the property will be worth after the work is completed.

The Basic Structure

1. **Future (As-Completed) Value.** The lender evaluates the value of your home after the ADU is built.
2. **Single Mortgage.** One loan covers:
    - The existing home
    - The cost of construction
3. **Funds Held in Escrow.** The renovation portion of the loan is not given to you upfront.
4. **Draws During Construction.** Funds are released to your contractor in stages as work is completed and inspected.

What This Solves. Renovation loans help overcome equity and credit barriers—not time or paperwork barriers.

The FHA 203(k) Loan: Access Over Simplicity

The **FHA 203(k)** is insured by the Federal Housing Administration and was created to encourage rehabilitation of older housing.

It is often the **most accessible renovation loan**—and also the most restrictive.

Why Some ADU Builders Choose the FHA 203(k)

- **Lower Credit Score Requirements.** Some lenders allow scores as low as 620.
- **Low Down Payment (for purchases).** As little as 3.5% down.
- **Based on Future Value.** Like construction loans, it uses an as-completed appraisal.

The FHA 203(k) exists to expand access—not to simplify construction.

The Tradeoffs You Must Accept

- **Mortgage Insurance for Life.** FHA loans require both upfront and monthly mortgage insurance, regardless of equity.
- **Strict Project Rules.** Not all ADU configurations or features are allowed.
- **Two Versions:**
    - Limited 203(k): Small projects (under ~$35,000)
    - Standard 203(k): Required for most ADUs

Most ADU projects will require the **Standard 203(k).**

The Fannie Mae Homestyle Loan: More Flexibility, Higher Bar

The **HomeStyle loan** is a conventional renovation loan backed by Fannie Mae.

It offers **more flexibility** than the FHA 203(k), but usually requires **stronger borrower qualifications.**

Why Homestyle Appeals to ADU Builders

- **Broader Project Eligibility.** Allows a wider range of improvements, including ADUs.
- **No FHA-Style Lifetime Mortgage Insurance.** PMI may be required if equity is under 20%, but it can be removed later.
- **Future-Value Based.** Uses an as-completed appraisal like other renovation loans.

> **The Middle Ground.** HomeStyle sits between FHA access and conventional discipline.

The Oversight Factor: The HUD Consultant (and Why It Matters)

Renovation loans come with **built-in oversight.**

For a **Standard FHA 203(k)**, you must hire a **HUD-approved 203(k) Consultant.**

This person works for the **lender**, not for you.

What the HUD Consultant Does

1. **Work Write-Up.** Creates a detailed scope of work and cost breakdown.
2. **Contractor Vetting.** Ensures your contractor meets program requirements.
3. **Inspections & Draw Approval.** Verifies progress before funds are released.

Homestyle loans don't always require a HUD consultant, but lenders still impose:

- Detailed documentation
- Strict inspections
- Controlled draw schedules

Renovation loans replace borrower flexibility with institutional control.

Pros and Cons: The Honest Tradeoff

Pros

- Lower credit score requirements
- Lower down payment (especially FHA)
- Based on future value
- Can unlock ADU financing when other loans won't

Cons

- Slow approval timelines
- Heavy paperwork
- Rigid draw process
- Additional consultant fees
- Limited contractor choice

Reality Check. These loans reward patience, not speed.

Who Renovation Loans Are Best For

Renovation loans make sense if you:

- Can't qualify for equity-based or construction loans
- Are willing to accept oversight and bureaucracy
- Have time for a longer approval process
- Need future-value underwriting to make the project work

They may be a poor fit if you:

- Want speed and flexibility
- Plan to self-manage construction
- Are uncomfortable with third-party control

Is a Renovation Loan Worth Exploring?

- ☐ I don't qualify for traditional ADU financing
- ☐ I'm comfortable with heavy documentation
- ☐ I can work within strict construction rules
- ☐ I have a contractor willing to meet program requirements
- ☐ I value access over convenience

If several boxes are unchecked, look elsewhere first.

Immediate Actions

1. **Confirm your credit score and down payment options**
2. **Ask lenders if ADUs are eligible under their renova-**

tion programs

3. **Verify your contractor's willingness to work under draws and inspections**
4. **Budget extra time and consultant costs**

Preparation is the difference between success and burnout.

Scripts You Can Use With Lenders

Script: Opening the Conversation

"Do you offer FHA 203(k) or HomeStyle loans for ADU construction?"

Script: Clarifying Requirements

"What restrictions apply to ADUs under this program?"

Script: Contractor Reality Check

"Will my contractor need to be approved, and how?"

Red-Flag Answer

"We'll figure that out once you apply."

With renovation loans, **details first—applications second.**

Government-backed renovation loans are not shortcuts.

They are **access ramps.**

For homeowners locked out of traditional financing, they can provide the leverage needed to build an ADU—but only if you're willing to trade speed and simplicity for structure and compliance.

If you enter with clear expectations, patience, and the right team, these loans can turn a stalled ADU dream into a funded reality.

CHAPTER 9

FINDING A LENDER: THE RISE OF ADU-SPECIFIC LOAN PRODUCTS

Not long ago, financing an ADU felt like trying to explain a UFO sighting to a bank.

Most lenders:

- Didn't understand ADUs
- Didn't trust the valuation
- Didn't know how to underwrite the risk

As a result, many homeowners were told "No"—not because their project was bad, but because the lender wasn't equipped to evaluate it.

That has changed.

The explosion in ADU construction has created a **new generation of lenders and loan products built specifically for this market**. Today, the challenge is no longer finding financing—it's choosing the **right** lender.

An ADU-friendly lender doesn't just approve loans faster—they prevent costly mistakes.

This chapter shows you **where to look, what to look for, and how to vet lenders like a professional.**

The New ADU Financing Landscape

While large national banks are still an option, many of the most effective ADU loans now come from **specialized and local institutions.**

Fintech Lenders: Designed for the Appraisal Gap

A new wave of technology-driven lenders has emerged to solve problems traditional banks struggled with—especially the appraisal gap.

These lenders often:

- Focus specifically on renovation and ADU projects
- Underwrite based on future (as-completed) value
- Use alternative structures traditional banks won't

Examples include companies like **RenoFi** and **Hometap**, which created products specifically for homeowners adding value through construction.

> **Why Fintech Matters.** These lenders didn't adapt old products—they built new ones for ADUs.

Local Credit Unions: Flexible and Relationship-Driven

Many California credit unions have quietly become **ADU financing experts.**

Their advantages:

- Local market knowledge
- More flexible underwriting
- Direct access to decision-makers

- Personalized service

In many cases, a credit union can approve an ADU loan that a national bank won't—even at similar rates.

Some of the best ADU loans in California never appear in online rate comparisons.

What Actually Makes a Lender "ADU-Friendly"

An attractive interest rate means nothing if the lender doesn't understand ADUs.

Here's what to look for instead.

1. Proven ADU Experience

Ask directly:

- How many ADU projects have you financed?
- In the last year?
- In my region?

A lender unfamiliar with ADUs will:

- Misunderstand permitting timelines
- Mis-handle appraisals
- Delay or deny draws

Experience prevents friction.

2. Product Flexibility

A strong ADU lender can offer:

- HELOCs
- Cash-out refinances

- Construction loans
- Renovation loans
- Hybrid or future-value products

You don't want a lender who says:

"This is the only product we offer."

3. Radical Transparency

A good lender should clearly explain:

- Interest rates (fixed vs. variable)
- Closing costs
- Draw procedures
- Appraisal method
- Contractor requirements

If explanations feel evasive or overly vague, that's a warning sign.

Red Flag

"We'll figure that out later" usually means you will pay for it later.

Why Pre-Approval Is Non-Negotiable

Before you finalize designs or hire a contractor, you should be **pre-approved by at least two to three lenders.**

Pre-approval is not the same as pre-qualification.

- **Pre-qualification** = rough estimate
- **Pre-approval** = conditional commitment

Pre-approval requires:

- Income verification
- Asset documentation
- Credit review
- Debt analysis

Why Pre-Approval Changes Everything

1. **It sets a real budget.** You design an ADU you can actually afford.
2. **It gives you leverage and speed.** When you choose a lender, most paperwork is already done.

Pre-approved borrowers don't guess—they decide.

Questions You Must Ask Every Potential Lender

Bring this list to every lender conversation.

Core Questions

- What ADU loan products do you offer?
- Do you underwrite based on current value or as-completed value?
- What are the minimum credit score and DTI requirements?
- What are the total closing costs?

Construction-Specific Questions

- How do construction draws work?
- Who performs inspections?
- What documentation is required before each draw?
- How do you approve contractors?

Timeline Questions

- Typical approval timeline?
- Typical appraisal timeline?
- Typical draw release timing?

If a lender struggles to answer these clearly, keep shopping.

Have You Found the Right Lender?

- ☐ The lender has financed ADUs before
- ☐ They offer more than one loan type
- ☐ They understand appraisal gaps
- ☐ They clearly explain fees and timelines
- ☐ You feel informed—not pressured

If any box is unchecked, don't commit yet.

Immediate Actions

1. **Identify at least three ADU-friendly lenders**
2. **Apply for pre-approval with at least two**
3. **Compare total cost, not just rate**

4. **Choose the lender who understands your project—not just your credit**

Scripts You Can Use With Lenders

Script: Opening the Conversation

"I'm planning an ADU and want to work with a lender experienced in ADU financing."

Script: Appraisal Clarity

"Is this loan based on current value or future as-completed value?"

Script: Draw Process

"How and when are construction funds released?"

Red-Flag Statement

"We don't do many ADUs, but it should be similar."

ADUs are never "similar."

The right lender doesn't just fund your ADU.

They:

- Anticipate problems
- Prevent delays
- Reduce stress
- Protect your timeline and budget

In ADU projects, financing is not a commodity—it's a partnership.

Choose accordingly.

CONCLUSION

BUILDING YOUR FINANCIAL ROADMAP

The journey to financing an Accessory Dwelling Unit can feel just as complex and intimidating as the construction itself, beginning with the anxiety of the $300,000 question and winding through credit scores, debt-to-income ratios, HELOCs, construction loans, renovation loans, and the appraisal gap, but the purpose of this book was simple: to replace anxiety with clarity—and now you have that clarity. What once felt like a maze is now a map, and more importantly, it's your map, tailored to your finances, your risk tolerance, and your goals, because homeowners who plan their financing before they design their ADU finish faster, spend less, and sleep better.

You now understand the primary financing paths available, from equity-based options like HELOCs and cash-out refinances, where the real choice is flexibility versus predictability, to construction-specific loans that unlock borrowing power based on future value and solve the appraisal gap when traditional lending falls short.

Financing an ADU is not about "finding money," but about choosing a structure that matches your reality, and turning that knowledge into action means assessing your true financial position, building an all-in budget that includes hard costs, soft costs, and a non-negotiable contingency, securing real pre-approval rather than hopeful estimates, selecting the loan that fits your situation, and managing cash flow during construction with the same discipline as the build itself. When you understand your borrowing limits, know your numbers, commit to a realistic budget, and manage the process deliberately, you move from thinking about an ADU to executing one.

An ADU is more than a building—it is a financial strategy, a housing solution, and an investment in your future—and now that you understand the rules of the game, the lenders, the limits, the leverage, and the risks, the project stops being a gamble and becomes a planned outcome. You have the roadmap, the tools, and the confidence—now go build, on purpose.

Made in United States
Troutdale, OR
11/03/2026

56844714R00056